ESSENTIAL

Finding Worth in Your Work
During Uncertain Times

A 30-day Devotional for Faith-Driven Workers

Brian Sooy

Scripture quotations marked (GW) are taken from the GOD'S WORD Translation,
copyright ©1995-2021 by God's Word to the Nations Mission Society. Used by
permission of God's Word to the Nations Mission Society. All rights reserved. Get
the Bible that brings God's saving truths to life for today's world at godsword.org.

Scripture quotations marked (NLT) are taken from the Holy Bible, New Living
Translation, copyright ©1996, 2004, 2015 by Tyndale House Foundation. Used by
permission of Tyndale House Publishers, a Division of Tyndale House Ministries,
Carol Stream, Illinois 60188. All rights reserved.

Cover and Interior Design by Aespire Brands | aespire.com

ESSENTIAL: Finding Worth in Your Work During Uncertain Times
ISBN: 978-1-954618-00-8 (Paperback) | ISBN: 978-1-954618-01-5 (eBook)

 Vide Press
6200 Second Street
Washington D.C. 20011
www.VidePress.com

First Printing 2021 in the United States of America

Visit EntreWorship.com for more inspiration and encouragement so you can
experience the joy of faith in your calling to the marketplace.

To the workers in the marketplace:
You're all essential.

Don't let anybody convince you otherwise.

"Who you are matters far more to God than what you do. Work is a precious gift from God, but it must not define who you are."

Foreword

Now more than ever, your work matters.

Why? Because our work is a means of glorifying God, loving neighbor as self, and revealing the kingship of Jesus Christ in every corner of creation. It's not enough to know that our work matters. We must "renew our minds" with what Scripture has to say about our work on a regular basis.

That's what this book aims to do and it is my pleasure to endorse this work.

Brian has done a terrific job of delivering a gospel-centric devotional that will remind you over the course of 30 days that your work matters to God. That your work is worship. To quote Brian, "You and I are to be co-creators with God, as a partner with him in his work to redeem the world."

This book will show you how and remind you of that truth on a daily basis.

> Jordan Raynor
> National bestselling author of
> *Called to Create* and *Master of One*

Preface

What does it mean to be essential?

"Stay at home. Shelter in place. You're not an essential worker."

I disagree.

We should never minimize the dedication and sacrifice of the front-line workers — healthcare personnel, first responders, the military, and others — who make other people's health and safety their first priority.

Every day the people who make it possible for us to live what we consider to be "normal" lives are labeled heroes — store workers, truck drivers, sanitation workers, and more.

"Hero" is how elected officials and the media label people are considered essential. At some point in our culture, when everybody gets to be a hero, nobody is a hero.

You may not think of yourself as a hero. Yet you are essential!

> *"Show me a hero, and I will write you a tragedy."*
> F. Scott Fitzgerald

Heroes are born out of tragedy, not out of everyday life. As much as we would love to believe that our work is heroic, we must manage our expectations and realize that the highest aspiration of our work is to be meaningful in ways that glorify God and for the good of others.

For the most part, our career choices don't require us to sacrifice our life or our property to create value for our customers, generate wealth, or provide for our families.

Yet the activity of work parallels the "hero act."

We go to work, we seek fulfillment, and then return home. Departure, fulfillment, return.

In many ways, the hero's journey reflects one of the deepest longings of the modern workforce, to work with a purpose.

In and of itself, is your work meaningful enough to help you find the sense of purpose that will fulfill you?

> *"A hero is someone who has given his life to something bigger than himself or other than himself."*
> JOSEPH CAMPBELL, *THE POWER OF MYTH*

Do you aspire to give your life to something greater or more significant than yourself, and if so, what cause is worthy of that desire?

We live in a world flawed by tragedy. All of creation was perfectly and beautifully spoken into existence and broken by disobedience and rebellion.

When all seemed lost, God offered hope.

In this story, Jesus is the hero in the grand act of redemption. Jesus gave his life for God's glory and your good.

> *"All heroes are shadows of Christ."*
> JOHN PIPER, *DON'T WASTE YOUR LIFE*

You and I are to be co-creators with God, as a partner with him in his work to redeem the world. We don't have to be the hero because one was given and gave his life to something bigger than himself.

As a Christ-follower, your role isn't to be the hero, but to be a guide who points people to Jesus. Your responsibility is to be an ambassador who recognizes Jesus as the hero.

Your calling is to fulfill your role as an irreplaceable and essential member of the body of Christ. The path you follow qualifies you to be the one the people need to guide them to the next milestone in their journey.

Be confident as you live and work in the shadow of the one true hero who saved the day for all eternity.

God calls people like you to guide people to Jesus, and that makes you essential.

* * *

Father, thank you for the hope and confidence I find only and always in Jesus Christ my Savior. I want the work you called me to do to be meaningful, and my life to be fulfilling. Help me be a person who is essential to the people around me. Amen.

THE ONE THING WE ALL NEED RIGHT NOW

If there's one thing we need right now, it's hope. Hope for today, for tomorrow, for the future.

Our families are isolated, our businesses are in duress, our stress levels are higher than ever. Where we were confident, now we're cautious. Where there was courage, now there is fear. Where we felt safe, now we feel threatened.

Even when we feel lost or like the path isn't well-marked, God tells us how to find the path to hope.

It's simple and may remind you of a song that was popular several years ago: *Don't Worry, Be Happy*.

> "**Don't worry** about anything,
> pray about everything.
> Tell God what you need,
> and thank him for what he's done."
> (PHILIPPIANS 4:6, *NEW LIVING TRANSLATION*)

Skeptical about that command? Take him at his word. *Trust him.*

> "*My brothers and sisters, **be very happy** when you are tested in different ways. You know that such testing of your faith produces endurance. Endure until your testing is over. Then you will be mature and complete, and you won't need anything.*"
> (JAMES 1:2-4, *GOD'S WORD TRANSLATION*)

Sound trite? Think about it.

The journey to hope follows the path of testing and suffering.

The Apostle Paul was no stranger to suffering. In the letter to the Romans, he wrote:

- Suffering creates endurance and perseverance,
- Endurance creates character and strength,
- Character creates confidence and hope.

Trust God. You're already on the journey. Follow the path.

Be grateful for the companions who travel this road with you toward our blessed hope.

Hope is what we all need right now, and hope does not disappoint.

* * *

Ask yourself:
What worry can I give to God today so I can have peace?

_____

_____

_____

_____

_____

For reflection:
Father, you remind us in Paul's letter to Timothy that we should trust in you, who richly gives us all we need for our enjoyment. When you test me, I know it's because you want to create endurance, perseverance, character, and strength in me, and confident hope in you! Amen.

Is Your Worth in What You Do?

*"The work of Beethoven and the work of a
charwoman become spiritual on precisely the same
condition, that of being offered to God. This does
not, of course, mean that it is for anyone a mere
toss-up whether he should sweep floors or compose
symphonies. We are members of one body, but
different members with his own vocation."*
C.S. Lewis, The Weight of Glory

What is it that you do?
- Do you think of yourself as an executive, business owner, or manager?
- Are you an artist, entrepreneur, an innovator?
- Are you a first responder, police officer, armed services member, or veteran?
- Do you drive a truck, push a broom, stock shelves, or serve food?

Are any of these vocations more valuable than the others?

No. God gave them all as gifts to the body of Christ, and each is essential.

By serving well in the role to which you're called you are helping build something greater.

You are more than the role you fill or the position you hold. If you think solely of your vocation, you possibly limit yourself and God's work to transform you and other people through you.

When you think of your job or vocation as something that only fulfills your need, you may be disappointed. When you believe your work, vocation, or role is precisely that to which God calls, you can be confident in its worth because you are an essential member of the body of Christ.

Your job is a spiritual gift from God that empowers you to meet the needs of others.

That alone should set you free. No matter where you serve, you are fulfilling your calling!

Who you are matters far more to God than what you do. Work is a precious gift from God, but it must not define who you are.

> *"Each of you as a good manager must use the gift that God has given you to serve others."*
> 1 PETER 4:10-11 GW

What is the Apostle Peter saying? Speak with authority. Serve powerfully. *Why?* Because even the one who sweeps the floors brings glory to God.

* * *

Ask yourself:
When the government declares some jobs essential and others "non-essential," what does the Lord say about your role in the body of Christ?

_____

_____

_____

_____

CALLING AND CONTENTMENT

I once met a man named Lawrence, who shines shoes and greets you like a friend.

"What's your name? My name is Lawrence."

Lawrence has been shining shoes since he was 11 years old. He shined shoes for Dean Martin and Sammy Davis Jr. (when a top-of-the-line shine paid 95¢ a pair, Martin paid him $20 a pair).

When you ask Lawrence, "How's business?" he responds, "It's OK, it's OK. I'm not worried; I'm just thankful for who God has brought to me today. He's giving me what I need."

Lawrence knows his business and does it well. He's at peace with his role, understands his calling, and focuses on contentment.

He embodies every word of this verse:

> *"Don't worry about anything; instead, pray about everything. Tell God what you need, and thank him for all he has done."*
> PHILIPPIANS 4:6 *NLT*

While his business may be shining shoes, Lawrence understands his calling, impacting his perspective on life.

When this man isn't shining shoes, he's shining souls.

Worrying doesn't change the outcome. Work is a gift from our generous God who gives us everything we need.

* * *

Ask yourself:
Would I feel content if God called me to shine shoes?

_____

_____

_____

_____

_____

For reflection:
Pray through these verses:

"Don't worry about anything; instead, pray about everything. Tell God what you need, and thank him for all he has done. Then you will experience God's peace, which exceeds anything we can understand. His peace will guard your hearts and minds as you live in Christ Jesus.

And now, dear brothers and sisters, one final thing. Fix your thoughts on what is true, and honorable, and right, and pure, and lovely, and admirable. Think about things that are excellent and worthy of praise. Keep putting into practice all you learned and received from me—everything you heard from me and saw me doing. Then the God of peace will be with you."

PHILIPPIANS 4:6-9 *NLT*

The True Meaning of Freedom

When we celebrate freedom, we think that sets us free to pursue our plans and dreams.

Then God gives us a different perspective to consider:

> *"In the same way, brothers and sisters, you have died to the laws in Moses' Teachings through Christ's body. You belong to someone else, the one who was brought back to life. As a result, we can do what God wants."*
>
> Romans 7:4 *GW*

Freedom is not about doing what you want to do.

Freedom is not an unrestricted license to pursue your passions.

God set you free from sin and death so that you can be free to serve others in love.

Here are four ways to experience the freedom God promised you:

1. Love God with your entire being because of all he's done for you,
2. Love everybody as you love yourself,
3. Choose what is good; turn away from what is evil,
4. Obey fearlessly so you can live in freedom.

Unattainable? *No.*
Challenging? *Yes.*

If living in freedom was easy, everybody would be doing it.

You have the power of Jesus Christ and the presence of the Holy Spirit living in you.

You are free to enjoy doing the good works God created you for and serving the people around you in love.

That's what freedom is all about.

* * *

Ask yourself:
Do I use my freedom to do what I want or pursue what God desires?

_____

_____

_____

_____

_____

For reflection:
Father, I always thought freedom was about me, but you revealed that freedom is all about you. Give me the strength to do the good works you planned for me and obey you fearlessly. Amen.

Beyond the Brokenness

I read one sentence this past weekend that made me stop and reflect that we often focus on our suffering instead of our flourishing:

> *"Redemption is what we ought to be celebrating, not constantly reminding ourselves of the crucifixion."*
> Bob Woodson

We celebrate redemption in life so we can experience the full joy of our faith.

How do we experience that celebration at work?

Despite what the media tells us, there is no "new normal." There is God's idea of normal; everything else is broken and unnatural. That can make the challenges you face at work feel overwhelming.

If we never move beyond what's broken, we'll never experience what's possible. We must work with the confident faith that our activities help God redeem the world and remember that he empowers us as partners in redemption.

- There is no redemption without the resurrection.
- If we only focus on what's broken (the crucifixion), we'll never experience what's possible (redemption) because of what is accomplished (the resurrection).
- The truth of the resurrection will never change; our roles and the world in which we live will always present new challenges.

Don't give up. Your work matters and you are an irreplaceable member of the body of Christ!

On the days your work feels meaningless, and you feel unimportant, remember: Because Christ died for you and rose from the dead, you have the power to celebrate the joy of your faith in the work God called you to do!

* * *

Ask yourself:
How can I experience the full joy of my faith at work?

_____

_____

_____

_____

_____

For reflection:
Father, thank you for the cross and Jesus' suffering. I rejoice in the resurrection and the power of the cross over sin and death. Thank you for redeeming me and giving me the freedom and opportunity to experience the full joy of faith in every moment of my life. Amen.

BE RELENTLESS

Sunday reminds us of the victory of the Cross, the power of the Resurrection, and God's sovereignty over every part of our life and work.

We need that good news because on Monday, it's *back to work*. Guiding your organization, leading your team, serving with excellence, doing the work God called you to.

At kitchen tables, home offices, in co-working spaces, or the office, you work to make an eternal difference for the glory of God and the good of others.

What are the three things you can do to overcome a disrupted routine?

Stay focused:

> *"Pay careful attention to your own work, for then you will get the satisfaction of a job well done, and you won't need to compare yourself to anyone else. For we are each responsible for our own conduct."*
> GALATIANS 6:4-5, *NLT*

You changed how you work overnight and must adapt to extraordinary circumstances. Perhaps you've been asked to go above and beyond yourself. Sunday worship was refreshing, but you still need strength and endurance to work as worship.

Don't give up:

> "We can't allow ourselves to get tired of living the right
> way. Certainly, each of us will receive everlasting life
> at the proper time, if we don't give up. Whenever we
> have the opportunity, we have to do what is good for
> everyone, especially for the family of believers."
> GALATIANS 6: 9-10, *NLT*

Be Relentless: You will get through this in the power of the
Resurrection!

* * *

Ask yourself:
What are two specific things I must do to stay strong when
doing good for others is more draining than refreshing?

_____

_____

_____

_____

_____

For reflection:
Father, remind me daily that the opportunity to work from home
is a blessing. Fill me with joy whether I'm talking with people
face-to-face or through a camera. I acknowledge that my work, no
matter where and when I do it, is worship. Amen.

SIMPLY BECAUSE

Have you ever noticed how many times the word "because" appears in the Psalms?

"Give thanks to the Lord *because* he is good,
  because his mercy endures forever...
...I give thanks to you,
  because you have answered me.
  You are my savior."
(from Psalm 118: 1, 21, *GW*)

"I will eagerly pursue your commandments
  because you continue to increase my understanding...
...Lead me on the path of your commandments,
  because I am happy with them.
...I will walk around freely
  because I sought out your guiding principles."
(from Psalm 119, *GW*)

Where does the word "because" lead us?
To the cross. To Jesus. To God's kindness and grace.

> *"But God is rich in mercy because of his great love for us.*
> *We were dead because of our failures, but he made us*
> *alive together with Christ.*
> *(It is God's kindness that saved you.)"*
> EPHESIANS 2:4-5 *GW*

When we live righteous lives and seek God's way, we experience the joy of faith, because that's what our loving Father wants for us.

* * *

Ask yourself:
How can I be more intentional in my relationship with God and experience his kindness?

_____

_____

_____

_____

_____

For reflection:
Lord, thank you for reminding us that we are your children because of your love for us. Amen!

THE SERVANT WITH NO NAME

Did you ever notice that the servant Abraham entrusted with choosing a wife for Isaac is never named?

He understood his role to serve Abraham, even in prayer.

He prayed for God to bless Abraham, with a specific request that asks for a specific response.

> "Then he prayed, "Lord, God of my master Abraham, make me successful today. Show your kindness to Abraham. Here I am standing by the spring, and the girls of the city are coming out to draw water. I will ask a girl, 'May I please have a drink from your jar?' If she answers, 'Have a drink, and I'll also water your camels,' let her be the one you have chosen for your servant Isaac. This way I'll know that you've shown your kindness to my master."
>
> GENESIS 24:12-15 GW

We can learn much from this servant — his prayer, his deep faith, his love for the one he served.

He is a model for anyone who feels their work goes unnoticed.

Don't be discouraged — your insight and expertise are critical and valuable — to your organization, leadership, staff, and the people whom you serve.

* * *

Ask yourself:
Jesus, am I really doing what I'm supposed to be doing?
Does my work make a Kingdom difference?

_____

_____

_____

_____

_____

For reflection:
The man knelt, bowing to the LORD with his face touching the ground. He said, "Praise the LORD, the God of my master Abraham. The LORD hasn't failed to be kind and faithful to my master. The LORD has led me on this trip to the home of my master's relatives."
GENESIS 24:26-27 *GW*

Lord, today I pray for the business leaders who intercede for success on behalf of the people they serve. Make them successful and show them how they are vessels of your unfailing love. Amen!

You Don't Need Permission

Are you asking yourself, "Does my work make a Kingdom difference?"

It's a valid question to get answers for when you view it through a different lens.

Let's take a look at Joseph, son of Israel, and how he served:

- Potiphar "...liked Joseph so much that he made him his trusted servant. He put him in charge of his household and everything he owned. From that time on the Lord blessed the Egyptian's household because of Joseph. Therefore, the Lord's blessing was on everything Potiphar owned in his house and in his fields. *So he left all that he owned in Joseph's care. He wasn't concerned about anything* except the food he ate." (Genesis 39:4-6 *GW*)

- Wrongfully accused, the Lord's favor was with Joseph, even in prison. The warden "...placed Joseph in charge of all the prisoners who were in that prison. Joseph became responsible for everything that they were doing. The warden *paid no attention to anything under Joseph's care* because the Lord was with Joseph and made whatever he did successful." (Genesis 39:22 *GW*)

During the best and worst of times during his life, Joseph focused on doing what pleased God. He pursued his responsibilities with excellence, and with God's favor, became a trusted servant whom leaders counted on.

Instead of asking, "Does my work make a Kingdom difference," what if you confidently declare how your work equips

others to make a Kingdom difference?
- I make a Kingdom difference when I offer wise guidance to people who look to me for leadership,
- I make a Kingdom difference when I equip and empower people to achieve their life goals and pursue God's will,
- I make a Kingdom difference when my work enables other leaders, the people with whom I work, and my family, to fulfill their calling.

When you show up every day to serve your Lord, you make a Kingdom difference.

You don't ever need permission to make a difference, so what are you waiting for?

The answers to the question are all around you.

* * *

Ask yourself:
How does my work equip and empower others to make a Kingdom difference?

_____

_____

_____

_____

_____

For reflection:
Father, you keep reminding me that there are two sides to obedience: pleasing you and serving others. I know I don't have to wait for permission to make a difference for you and your kingdom. Amen!

You're Never Alone

If there is one thing that CEOs, entrepreneurs, and leaders share in common, it's the feeling of isolation and loneliness that is a constant companion for the role.

When you are forced to work from home and separated from your coworkers, you may feel the same way. Video chat and phone calls are no substitute for face-to-face interaction.

Psalm 13 expresses the frustration and hope we're all feeling right now and the question you're thinking in your heart:

> *"How long, O Lord? Will you forget me forever?*
> *How long will you hide your face from me?*
> *How long must I make decisions alone*
> *with sorrow in my heart day after day?*
> *How long will my enemy triumph over me?"*
> PSALM 13:1-2, GW

1 & 2 Kings and the Psalms show us this: David turned to God for direction in everything.

> *"Look at me! Answer me, O Lord my God!*
> *Light up my eyes,*
> *or else I will die*
> *and my enemy will say, "I have overpowered him."*
> *My opponents will rejoice because I have been shaken."*

"Light up my eyes..." When you turn your eyes to our Lord, does it revive you?

"But I trust your mercy.
My heart finds joy in your salvation.
I will sing to the Lord because he has been good to me."
  (PSALM 13:1-2, *GW*)

David was confident in one thing above all others: *He trusted in God to deliver him.*

* * *

Ask yourself:
To be reliant, am I turning to God for direction in every decision I make?

_____

_____

_____

_____

_____

For reflection:

A person may plan his own journey,
but the Lord directs his steps.
PROVERBS 16:9 *GW*

The Lord is the one who directs a person's steps.
How then can anyone understand his own way?
PROVERBS 20:24 *GW*

THE PRACTICAL PRESENCE OF GOD

In the book of Exodus, "The Lord would speak to Moses personally, as a man speaks to his friend."

Wow! We know God as the Creator, Redeemer, Almighty, Everlasting, and more. His desire is we are confident in our relationship so we can talk with him as a friend.

A prayer for when you talk to God as you would to a friend:

On days like this and in uncertain times, I thank you, almighty God, that our Lord Jesus Christ rescues me! You assure me that those who believe in Christ Jesus can no longer be condemned, and that gives me great comfort.

I know that all things work together for the good of those who love you—people like me whom you called according to your plan. What can I say about all of this?

I boldly and confidently proclaim: "If God is for me, who can be against me?"

I know you love me and give me an overwhelming victory in all my difficulties and all the plans you created me for. Thank you for revealing the riches of your glory by making me the object of your mercy while you prepare me for glory.

My faith comes from hearing the message, and the message that I heard is what Christ spoke.

Everything is from you and by you and for you.

Glory belongs to you forever!

Amen.

Based on Romans 7:25, Romans 8:1, Romans 8:28, Romans 8:3, Romans 8:37, Romans 10:17, and Romans 11:36, GOD'S WORD Translation.

* * *

Ask yourself:

What is God saying to you today, right now, as a friend?

_____

_____

_____

_____

_____

For reflection:

"When all the people saw the column of smoke standing at the entrance to the tent, they would all bow with their faces touching the ground at the entrance to their own tents. The Lord would speak to Moses personally, as a man speaks to his friend. Then Moses would come back to the camp, but his assistant, Joshua, son of Nun, stayed inside the tent.

Moses said to the Lord, "You've been telling me to lead these people, but you haven't let me know whom you're sending with me. You've also said, 'I know you by name, and I'm pleased with you.'"

EXODUS 33:10-12, *GW*

DON'T BE A DULL BLADE

*"As iron sharpens iron, so one person
sharpens the wits of another."*
PROVERBS 27:17 *GW*

When you've been on the go, sometimes you feel like you've been dulled by the constant grind of life, like a knife set at the wrong angle against a sharpening stone.

The writer of this proverb could have meant several things when they wrote it. Many translations are vague in their translation; this particular translation focuses on the "wits of another."

Does that mean humor? Mental sharpness? Situational awareness? Or does it refer to our relationships and conversations?

Most likely, *it's all of the above.*

We need each other for accountability, motivation, problem-solving, and community.

God designed you to be an essential and integral part of the body of Christ. We help each other do better work and fulfill our calling to Christ.

We limit our growth when we only surround ourselves with people whose experiences and perspectives agree with our preconceptions, beliefs, and biases.

The people with whom you spend time will sharpen or dull you, draw you closer or drive you further away from a relationship with God, and enlighten or confuse you.

Choose wisely and invest your time well. You can learn much more about your calling and how God values your work by spending time with like-minded believers and professionals.

What's more, you will be a guide to others who are desperate to know that their work is meaningful, their calling is necessary, and that God loves them for who they are, not what they do.

Either way, you're part of the process. You stay sharp by remembering this one truth:

When iron sharpens iron – sometimes you're the hammer – and sometimes you're the blade.

* * *

Ask yourself:
Am I authentic and transparent with the people around me?

_____

_____

_____

_____

_____

For reflection:
Lord, surround me with people who will sharpen me. Connect me with people whom I can encourage and disciple. Remind us that we are essential to each other and to your church, the body of Christ. Amen!

WE'RE BETTER TOGETHER

We can't seek solutions or expect to find answers to any of the problems we face without hearing the words the Holy Spirit whispers into our hearts and minds.

> *"You mortals, the Lord has told you what is good.*
> *This is what the Lord requires from you:*
> *to do what is right, to love mercy,*
> *and to live humbly with your God."*
> — MICAH 6:8 *GW*

When we stand with God, we take our stand alongside mercy and truth:

> *"Righteousness and justice are the foundations of your*
> *throne. Mercy and truth stand in front of you."*
> PSALM 89:14, *GW*

The beauty of the body of Christ is in its diversity of gifts, skills, thought, and experience. When we stand together, we are more resilient as a body.

As you continue to navigate a future that often seems uncertain, you need the body of Christ to remind you that we are better together.

- We strengthen each other.
- We encourage each other.
- We learn from each other.
- We are dependent on each other.

As Paul prayed, "We ask this so that you will live the kind of lives that prove you belong to the Lord. Then you will want to please him in every way as you grow in producing every kind of good work by this knowledge about God. We ask him to strengthen you by his glorious might with all the power you need to patiently endure everything with joy. You will also thank the Father, who has made you able to share the light, which is what God's people inherit." (Colossians 1:10-12 *GW*)

As a body, we're stronger together, and we're better together.

* * *

Ask yourself:
How can I strengthen the body of Christ today by creating or nurturing a relationship?

_____

_____

_____

_____

_____

For reflection:
Father, I choose to stand with you today. I commit to doing what is right and what pleases you. Teach me to love mercy and show me how to live humbly with you. Amen.

DEPENDING ON ME

The word that comes to mind when I think about dependence on God is, "reliant."

From the provision of manna to the Lord's prayer, God's reminder to his children is, "Depend on Me."

> *"He was the one who fed you in the desert with manna,*
> *which your ancestors had never seen. He did this in*
> *order to humble you and test you. But he also did this*
> *so that things would go well for you in the end."*
> DEUTERONOMY 8:16, *GW*

Not only does God ask us to depend on him, he often surprises us with resources and leads us on paths we "had never seen."

Imagine how terrified the nation of Israel was with the Dead Sea in front of them and the Egyptians in close pursuit behind them.

God told Moses to lead them through the sea, and Moses told them to follow:

> *"Your road went through the sea.*
> *Your path went through raging water,*
> *but your footprints could not be seen."*
> PSALM 77:19, GW

Why does he ask us to depend on him?

"So that things would go well for you in the end."

When you're a child of God — He does ALL things for his purpose and his glory — and your benefit.

When it appears that God is asking you to trust and be unwaveringly reliant, depend on him.

* * *

Ask yourself:
Where can I depend on God more and less on my credentials, skills, and abilities?

_____

_____

_____

_____

_____

For reflection:
Lord, as I work this week, show me how to lift thanksgiving and praise you for your unfailing love and unlimited provision, and remind me you are a God of generosity and not scarcity whose power is made perfect in my weakness. Amen.

ABUNDANCE OR SCARCITY?

A re you satisfied with the life God's given you, or are you continually seeking just a bit more?

> *"A godly life brings huge profits to people who are content with what they have. We didn't bring anything into the world, and we can't take anything out of it. As long as we have food and clothes, we should be satisfied."*
> 1 TIMOTHY 6:6-8 *GW*

Our glorious God is generous. He created an abundance of resources for us. If we focus on what's lacking, we may miss out on the blessing of seeing God's abundant provision.

You have the choice to approach each day with
• An abundance mentality, (an optimistic view), or
• A scarcity mentality (a cautious view).

Believing you have enough is critical to the joy you experience at work, at home, and in your relationship with God.

What do you need that God hasn't already given you?

What if you focused on what you have instead of the constant longing for what you don't have?

When you do, you can stop comparing yourself to people around you and cease being envious of their achievements.

You are equipped with all you need, but if you don't recognize that God gave you everything you need for living a godly life, you'll never be satisfied with anything.

You can't carry around the weight of other people's

perceived expectations and expect to run this race well. You don't have to let culture define your identity or performance expectations. You don't have to set personal expectations so high that you never meet them.

> *"God's divine power has given us everything we need*
> *for life and for godliness. This power was given to us*
> *through knowledge of the one who called us by his own*
> *glory and integrity. Through his glory and integrity he*
> *has given us his promises that are of the highest value."*
> 2 Peter 1:3-4 GW

You don't have anything to prove, and certainly nothing to lose, because the victory is won!

God's provision is always enough, no matter the situation.

* * *

Ask yourself:

What will change in my outlook if I live each day with confidence in God's provision?

_____

_____

_____

_____

_____

For Reflection:

Lord, I confess that when my eyes are on what I expect from myself that I'm always disappointed. Help me keep my eyes on Jesus, knowing he fulfilled your expectations for me. Amen.

BOTH/AND

When you're miles down a trail, you have to look behind you to see how far you've come and what you accomplished.

Your career is like that. You can look back with thanks for all the good things God has done for you and accomplished through you as you serve people with excellence.

It's easy to stray from the path. Every day, we must pray:

"Make your ways known to me, O Lord,
and teach me your paths.
Lead me in your truth and teach me
because you are God, my savior.
I wait all day long for you."
    PSALM 25:4-5, *GW*

"As for me, since I am poor and needy,
let the Lord keep me in his thoughts.
You are my helper and my savior.
O my God, do not delay."
    PSALM 40:17, *NLT*

We live in constant tension:
- We know we're "poor and needy," as the Psalmist proclaims at the end of Psalm 40.
- God commands us to be strong and courageous as he told Joshua multiple times in Deuteronomy 31.

Which should it be?

Not either/or.

We're both/and.

We can be *both* poor and needy *and* strong and courageous in Christ when we are dependent on Him.

* * *

Ask yourself:

What are the good things God does for me for which I can give thanks every day?

_____

_____

_____

_____

_____

For reflection:

Father, ambiguity, and uncertainty fill me with worry, anxiety, and tension. I commit to walking the path of my life with humility and courage in the power of the Holy Spirit. Lord, keep me in your thoughts today. I want to be reliant on you. Amen!

Joy is Strength

Right now, you may be experiencing anger, frustration, worry, and a host of other emotions when what your heart desires most is joy.

Our heavenly Father knows what you need and how you can get it.

God desires to strengthen you with the joy he wants you to experience.

> *"We ask him to strengthen you by his glorious might with all the power you need to patiently endure everything with joy."*
> Colossians 1:11 *GW*

Let's break it down:
- We ask God to strengthen you,
- We ask God to strengthen you by his glorious might,
- We ask God to strengthen you all the power you need,
- We ask God to strengthen you to patiently endure everything,
- We ask God to strengthen you with joy.

Joy is strength.

Do you want more joy for yourself and those around you? Pray for strength!

* * *

Ask yourself:
Am I praying for strength or am I content to struggle in weakness?

_____

_____

_____

_____

_____

For reflection:
Father, strengthen me by your glorious might, with all the power I need so I can patiently endure everything with joy. I pray this for my family, friends, and co-workers who all need you. Amen!

THE ROI OF TRUST

There's so much benefit when you trust in the Lord and lean into his power and strength:

- *Trusting the Lord surrounds you with mercy:* "Many heartaches await wicked people, but mercy surrounds those who trust the Lord."

    PSALM 32:10 *GW*

- *Trusting the Lord results in blessing:* "Whoever gives attention to the Lord's word prospers, and blessed is the person who trusts the Lord."

    PROVERBS 16:20 *GW*

- *Trusting the Lord gives you confidence:* "Blessed is the person who trusts the Lord. The Lord will be his confidence."

    JEREMIAH 17:7 *GW*

- *Trusting God reduces fear:* "I praise God's word. I trust God. I am not afraid. What can mere flesh and blood do to me?"

    PSALM 56:4 *GW*

- *When you trust God, other people notice:* "He placed a new song in my mouth, a song of praise to our God. Many will see this and worship. They will trust the Lord."

    PSALM 40:3 *GW*

God made you who you are and created you in Christ Jesus to live a life filled with good works he prepared for you to accomplish.

You're not on your own.

You're not alone.

As the Psalmist reminds you Psalm 115:9-11, "...*trust the Lord. He is your helper and your shield.*"

* * *

Ask yourself:
What am I most afraid of today? How can I make the Lord my confidence in my fear?

_____

_____

_____

_____

For reflection:
Lord, I declare my trust in you, throwing all my worries at your feet. Hold my hand and shield me from the evil one. Amen!

INTO THE DEEP WATER

*"God has made us what we are. He has created us in
Christ Jesus to live lives filled with good works that he
has prepared for us to do."*
EPHESIANS 2:10 *GW*

Before Jesus invited Peter to walk on water, he gave him a more straightforward challenge.

In Luke 5, Jesus told Peter to change things up. Stop working the same way, and work outside of your comfort zone. Change the status quo. Put out into the deep water.

Peter feared the deep — where are you afraid of where God wants you to go?

When Jesus calls you to leave the safety of the shore and go into the deep water of life, how do you respond?

When God tells you that he created us to do good works, we must also keep in mind Psalm 32:7:

*"I will instruct you.
I will teach you the way that you should go.
I will advise you as my eyes watch over you."*

We're often so short-sighted in our faith. Peter worked hard all night and caught nothing. Did he push off from the shore after sitting in the Savior's presence with little expectation of different results?

When you work hard and don't experience the results you anticipate, how do you respond when the Lord says, "Try it this way"?

Why would Peter continue to work the same way as he had in the past when it didn't produce results?

What did Peter's coworkers think as he led them into possible danger? What was Peter expecting?

The next time Peter was out in deep water (in Matthew 14), he could have been satisfied with walking on water, yet gave in to his fear.

In both stories, Jesus was present in the boat or on the water. He invites us to put out into the deep, walk on water, and experience abundant life.

Step out of the boat with courage and in faith.

Abundant life begins with an empty net.

* * *

Ask yourself:
Am I reluctant to change the way I work because I am afraid I might succeed?

_____

_____

_____

_____

For reflection:
Lord, I know my faith is a celebration! Don't let me expect less when Jesus offers abundance in my walk with him and the freedom to go where he leads. Amen.

MAKING BETTER DECISIONS

M oses' advice for leaders who have important decisions
to make is as relevant today as when he spoke to Israel:

*"Be impartial in your decisions. Listen to the least
important people the same way you listen to the most
important people. Never be afraid of anyone, since your
decisions come from God."*
DEUTERONOMY 1:17 *GW*

What can you learn from Moses?
- **Seek to be impartial.** Unconsciously, we bring bias into
  every decision we make. Pray that the Lord will give you
  the wisdom to make decisions based on the facts and not
  feelings.
- **Listen to everybody.** Fred Rogers (of Mr. Roger's
  Neighborhood fame) slowed down and listened to every
  individual he interacted with every day, from the locker
  room attendant at his gym to the broadcast company
  president. You can't influence culture when you're in a
  hurry. You make better decisions when you listen to multiple perspectives.
- **Never be afraid.** You're never going to make the right
  decision 100% of the time. If you allow fear of making
  the wrong decision to paralyze you, nothing will ever
  get done. Ask God for wisdom for every decision and be
  courageous.

* * *

Ask yourself:
How can I be more reliant on God when I make decisions?

_____

_____

_____

_____

_____

For reflection:
Father, give me the wisdom to make decisions based on facts and centered on trusting you for insight and guidance. Help me slow down so I can listen to those around me who need my help. Guide me with your wisdom and insight this week. Allow me the grace to be impartial, the time to be intentional in listening, and the courage to make decisions that align with your will. Amen.

TRAPPED BY OUR WORDS

Unsettled. Unprecedented. Impossible.
Do you feel trapped by the words other people use to describe today?

Do you catch yourself using words that make people feel like there's no hope?

> *"Let Christ's word with all its wisdom and richness live in you. Use psalms, hymns, and spiritual songs to teach and instruct yourselves about God's kindness. Sing to God in your hearts. Everything you say or do should be done in the name of the Lord Jesus, giving thanks to God the Father through him."*
> COLOSSIANS 3:16-17 *GW*

Wise advice: Let Christ's words live in you. Use the Word and songs of hope to teach yourself how to think. Speak in the name of the Lord, with thanks.

Right now, our culture is toxic. The Lord wants to speak through people like you to encourage the people around you with words that give them hope and inspire them to give thanks for God's kindness.

Don't believe everything that you hear. What God says about you and the world is more real than what you hear.

Listen to the words your heavenly Father speaks into your heart and mind, and believe them.

You don't have to live the story somebody else writes for you. Choose to believe the story God planned for you.

The words you believe should set you free!

* * *

Ask yourself:
Do the words I choose to use give people confidence in and point people to Jesus?

_____

_____

_____

_____

_____

For reflection:
Father, may the words I use be positive and uplifting. May they add flavor to conversations instead of bitterness. Fill my mind with words of hope and songs of faith. Amen.

How Long, O Lord?

I don't know about you, but I've reached my saturation point with news and mass media. *Enough already!*

When much of the news we read is so negative, how can we greet each day with joy?

Whenever I find myself getting cynical or discouraged, I turn back to this one verse:

> *"Finally, brothers and sisters, keep your thoughts on whatever is right or deserves praise: things that are true, honorable, fair, pure, acceptable, or commendable."*
> Philippians 4:8, *GW*

We can't ignore the news or the times in which we live. We are God's ambassadors who partner with him to redeem the culture in which we live.

We must be like the descendants of Issachar:

> *"From Issachar's descendants there were 200 leaders who understood the times and knew what Israel should do. "*
> 1 Chronicles 12:32, *GW*

We must learn to embrace the tension in which we live joyfully.

As a leader, you must understand the times and know what to do on behalf of the organization and the people you lead.

* * *

Ask yourself:
What am I doing to prepare myself and the people I lead for the future?

_____

_____

_____

_____

_____

For reflection:
Lord, help me to pay attention to what you are doing, understand the times, and to know what to do. Amen.

WHY YOU SHOULD LISTEN TO DREAMERS

A global poll revealed that only 15% of employees are engaged at work. It's slightly higher in the US, at 30%. That means two things:

- Only 15% of millions of workers find meaning in the work they are doing,
- An overwhelming 85% of people are dissatisfied with their job or their manager.

When you feel like your work doesn't matter, what can you do?

Your work has more meaning when you consider yourself part of the team.

After Joseph was released from prison and interpreted Pharaoh's dream, he displayed remarkable perspective:

> "This food will be a reserve supply for **our country** during the seven years of famine that will happen in Egypt. Then the land will not be ruined by the famine."
> GENESIS 41:36 GW

In this passage, Joseph identified himself as an Egyptian — not a captive or a servant — when he said, "our country."

Your work has two layers, whether you are a manager or an employee: to listen to dreamers and help interpret the dreams, so they succeed.

When your approach to your work is to listen and respond with your insight, intellect, experience, and wisdom, you provide the interpretation of how to solve a problem (a disturbing dream) or achieve a goal (a defining dream).

In this way, you will be like Joseph, allowing God to speak and work through you.

That's how you find meaning in the work you do every day and become one of the 15% who changes the future.

* * *

Ask yourself:
Do I think of myself as part of the team where I work?

_____

_____

_____

_____

_____

For reflection:
Father, on the days when my job isn't fulfilling, remind me that you gave me everything. Everything. Help me be content. Just like I'm an essential member of your church, the body of Christ, I'm part of a team helping other people grow, solve problems, and succeed in life. Amen.

CAN LEADERSHIP REALLY BE THIS SIMPLE?

Have we made leadership too complicated? The discipline of leadership is something to which many of us aspire yet struggle to practice.

We're reluctant to follow a path to leadership because we're not sure of the direction it will lead.

Leadership flows from obedience. Like we see with so many people in Scripture, our loving heavenly Father expands or limits our leadership opportunities to grow us and achieve his purposes.

The Apostle Peter offers this encouragement for reluctant leaders:

> *"Therefore, your minds must be clear and ready for action. Place your confidence completely in what God's kindness will bring you when Jesus Christ appears again."*
> 1 PETER 1:13 GW

What's he saying here? Think clearly, be prepared, have hope.

Think about it another way: Get clarity, have confidence, be ready to fulfill your calling.

The 'new normal' is your opportunity to model clear thinking and courageous action because God wants to show the world the spectacular things he does.

* * *

Ask yourself:

How can I give hope to the people I work with by reminding them that their work matters?

_____

_____

_____

_____

_____

For reflection:

When I hear your voice today, Lord, may my mind be clear, so I am ready to act when you call. I want to be confident in my role as a leader but am not always confident, which makes me reluctant to act. Help me be like your servant Joshua, whom you called to follow your commands and be strong and courageous. Give me faith and confidence in you because I know you do spectacular things. Amen.

What Type of Leader are You Becoming?

*"For God is working in you, giving you the desire and
the power to do what pleases him."*
Philippians 2:13 *NLT*

When it comes to the role you play at work and home, what type of leader are you becoming?

- *Are you humble,* recognizing your leadership is for the benefit of others?
- *Are you accessible,* making yourself available so you can equip people to do their best work for God's glory?
- *Are you aware* that your team is serving one another and the stakeholders in your organization?
- *Are you empowering, supporting, and equipping* everyone you meet and with whom you interact?
- *Are you full of grace*, recognizing that everyone is trying to survive and thrive, and nobody is perfect?

God cares about who you are and who you are becoming. He will make you more like Jesus and a beautiful, unique expression of what it means to be human.

Today is your moment to be more like and help others become more like Christ.

Ask yourself:
Which of the five qualities above makes me more like Jesus?

_____

_____

_____

_____

_____

For reflection:
Father, I know that your ultimate goal is for me to be more like Jesus — to be transformed and conformed — so you can point to me as an example of your kindness. Fill me with your Holy Spirit and empower me to point people to Jesus.

Lord, make me aware of the desire and purpose which you've put in me. When anxiety may be high and the future uncertain, help me be the type of leader Jesus was — and is — so that you are pleased. Amen.

VISION THAT WORKS

When he heard the news about his people and
Jerusalem's conditions, Nehemiah was literally in
shock. He wept and mourned for days.

Then he got to work.

- First, *Nehemiah prayed*. He began with a prayer of confession, repentance, and a request for favor from King
  Artaxerxes (Nehemiah 1:4-11) and prayed at every crucial
  moment when he knew he needed God's help.
- Next, *Nehemiah planned*. Without seeing the condition
  of the wall, Nehemiah knew what to do. No committees
  or stakeholder engagement. He was a leader and knew
  the time for buy-in would come. For now, the vision was
  to rebuild and restore the Israelite's dignity. After praying
  for favor again, he shared his plan, the timeline, and the
  specifics that would help him achieve his vision with the
  influencer who mattered, the King and his wife.
- To achieve his vision, *Nehemiah participated*. He showed
  us what it's like to maintain a posture of prayer while
  confidently getting things accomplished. Nehemiah was a
  leader who sought the Lord's favor from the beginning to
  the end of the process while he participated in the vision
  the Lord gave him.
- When his vision was accomplished, *Nehemiah prayed*:
  "Remember me for what I have done, my God, and don't
  wipe out the good things that I have done for your temple
  and for the worship that is held there."

Everything Nehemiah sought to accomplish was for the good of the people and the glory of God. Similarly, the work he planned for your life is for the body of Christ and your participation in the daily act of worship we call work.

We can't ask for a better motivation or model for our careers and calling.

Remember me for what I have done, my God. Amen!

* * *

Ask yourself:

Am I asking God to guide and direct me in the big and little plans of my life?

_____

_____

_____

_____

_____

For reflection:

Lord, there are four steps to being a confident and courageous leader like Nehemiah: Pray, plan, participate and pray. Let everything I do be for your glory and the good of the people you love. Amen.

LEADING THROUGH UNCERTAIN TIMES

When faced with a crisis, how do you respond? Panic? Calm? Measured? Focused?

It's important to remember that you are not on your own —you're part of a team— and the team must have a common purpose, a shared goal, and Christ-centered love for the people they serve.

You are a leader. People are looking to you to lead them with strength and courage.

It's human to be afraid. Joshua was probably scared as he stood at the border of the promised land. There is no courage without fear to overcome.

God knew that and him, "Be strong and courageous! Don't tremble or be terrified, because the Lord your God is with you wherever you go." (Joshua 1:9,)

With the confidence he gained from God's command, Joshua took charge. He laid out a plan. He cast the vision for what the future would look like if the people obeyed God.

Like Joshua, we can view the future as a desert of wandering or land of promise. Either way, it's an opportunity to be the leader God prepared you to be for a time like this.

The only way to respond to a crisis is by faith.

How will you respond today?

Ask yourself:
Am I a confident leader or a reluctant leader, and why?

_____

_____

_____

_____

_____

For reflection:
Lord, we give you thanks for the circumstances in which you place us and the opportunity you set before us. You promised to be with us. You are our strength, our confidence, our wisdom! Give us strength and courage in the face of our fear and help us lead our teams and our organization with the wisdom and confidence that flows from your loving heart. Amen!

"Be strong and courageous, because you will help these people take possession of the land I swore to give their ancestors.

"Only be strong and very courageous, faithfully doing everything in the teachings that my servant Moses commanded you. Don't turn away from them. Then you will succeed wherever you go. Never stop reciting these teachings. You must think about them night and day so that you will faithfully do everything written in them. Only then will you prosper and succeed.

"I have commanded you, 'Be strong and courageous! Don't tremble or be terrified, because the Lord your God is with you wherever you go.'"

JOSHUA 1:6-9 *GW*

GRACE OVER PRESSURE

Are leaders born or made? Leaders are refined and distilled over time. The distillation process involves heat and pressure, and the result is the essence of the opportunities, experiences, and time that went into it.

Heat and pressure are part of the process to break down and strengthen that which is weak.

When we turn to Jesus as a leadership model, we must remember that the pressure of growing up under an oppressive regime strengthened him for his ministry years.

> Jesus was *"...a man of sorrows, familiar with suffering.*
> *He was despised like one from whom people*
> *turn their faces, and we didn't consider*
> *him to be worth anything..."*
> ISAIAH 53:3 *GW*

Will you succumb to pressure, or rely on grace over weakness?

There will always be pressure on you. The weight of the past prepared you for the challenges you face today. Today's challenges prepare you to manage what comes next.

In every circumstance, God reminds you, "My grace is all you need. My power works best in weakness."

* * *

Ask yourself:
Where am I facing the most significant pressure now, and how is it strengthening me?

_____

_____

_____

_____

_____

For reflection:
    Lord, I know these tough times will pass. I'm doing the best I can to trust in you. Thank you for refining and strengthening me. I choose to let my circumstances strengthen my faith in you and your power to strengthen me to endure the circumstances I'm in. Amen.

Confidence in Uncertainty

P aul exhorts Timothy to share this with the people he
leads:

> "Tell those who have the riches of this world not to be
> arrogant and not to place their confidence in anything
> as uncertain as riches. Instead, they should place
> their confidence in God who richly provides us with
> everything to enjoy."
> 1 Timothy 6:17, GW

Was Paul thinking of us?

We all have access to resources of which Paul never
dreamed.

What are these riches to which Paul refers?

Riches go beyond material wealth to anything that threat-
ens to hold us captive.

What value is there in focusing on what is uncertain when
we can enjoy and flourish in what God gives us?

We shouldn't place our confidence in careers or calling,
only in Christ.

* * *

Ask yourself:
What riches does God give me so that I may enjoy my work
and role in the body of Christ?

_____

_____

_____

_____

_____

For reflection:
Lord, remind me every day that my job is a gift from you. Remind
me that to the body of Christ, I'm essential. Remind me that I
need to be reliant upon you. Amen.

"But you...must avoid these things. Pursue what God
approves of: a godly life, faith, love, endurance, and gentle-
ness. Fight the good fight for the Christian faith. Take hold of
everlasting life to which you were called and about which you
made a good testimony in front of many witnesses.

At the right time God will make this known. God is the
blessed and only ruler. He is the King of kings and Lord of
lords. He is the only one who cannot die. He lives in light that
no one can come near. No one has seen him, nor can they see
him. Honor and power belong to him forever! Amen."
1 TIMOTHY 6:11-12, 15-16, *GW*

WORK FOR THE GOOD

No matter what type of work you are doing, your vocation has significance and meaning.

When Babylon took Israel into exile, God spoke through Jeremiah:

> *"This is what the Lord of Armies, the God of Israel, says to all those who were taken captive from Jerusalem to Babylon: Build houses, and live in them. Plant gardens, and eat what they produce. Get married, and have sons and daughters. Find wives for your sons, and let your daughters get married so that they can have sons and daughters. Grow in number there; don't decrease.* **Work for the good of the city where I've taken you as captives, and pray to the Lord for that city. When it prospers, you will also prosper."*
> JEREMIAH 29:5 GW

Venture capitalist Sean Ammirati says, "It's easy to overlook the significance of the work you are doing, especially when we don't have a lens to fully appreciate its future impact."

We are all part of God's bigger plan to restore the world and to reconcile people to him.

Remember to pray and work for the good, peace, and prosperity of your city, region, state, and country so God can keep his promise of prosperity to us.

We accomplish the good works that God planned for us when we work for our cities' good and the people whom he loves.

* * *

Ask yourself:
How does the work I do now impact the future of my family and community?

_____

_____

_____

_____

_____

For reflection:
Lord, I pray for the prosperity of the business where I work and the community in which I live. Show me how I can work for the good of the city, and give me the courage to take the initiative where I see needs that I can meet. I know I may not see the results or impact of my work, but as long as you get the glory, that's what really matters. Amen.

About the Author

Brian Sooy is the president of Aespire (aespire.com), the branding and marketing agency that helps people build relationship brands that close the marketing gap.

As a StoryBrand Certified Guide, Brian helps business owners and entrepreneurs gain confidence that their marketing investment creates ROI and helps them grow their business.

Brian is recognized as one of Relevance.com's *Top 100 Marketing Influencers to Follow* and is the author of several books, including the top-rated *Raise Your Voice: A Cause Manifesto*, the top-rated guide for mission-driven leaders, and *Converge: A Journal about the Intersection of Work, Faith, and Worship*.

The devotionals in this book are inspired by EntreWorship, where you will find encouragement and wisdom from the Bible to help you experience the joy of work as worship and thrive in the marketplace.

Connect with Brian everywhere online:
- entreworship.com
- entreworship.com/subscribe
- linkedin.com/in/briansooy/
- twitter.com/briansooy
- aespire.com

ALSO BY BRIAN G. SOOY

Raise Your Voice: A Cause Manifesto

Many organizations struggle to attract, engage, and retain supporters. *Raise Your Voice* is a guidebook that empowers your cause to fulfill its promise and invite your donors to be part of the difference you make in people's lives.

This guidebook is full of practical insights for helping mission-driven organizations sustain a clear and focused mission, understand what motivates (and how to motivate) donors, build deeper relationships, and tell stories that resonate with people so they listen, care, act, and donate.

Converge: A Journal about the Intersection of Work, Faith, and Worship

Converge is a journal about working by faith, written for entrepreneurs and business leaders like you. God has given you a lifetime to explore where your purpose, calling, and vocation converge. EntreWorship® helps you make the most of the career to which you have been called.

Discover how faith-driven entrepreneurs align faith with work and fearlessly follow the narrow path.

Order all of Brian's books for entrepreneurs and business leaders at https://go.aespire.com/author-brian-sooy

Readers Respond to other books by Brian Sooy:

"Brian Sooy cares deeply about entrepreneurs and about Christ. This book shows how the two are so powerfully, and masterfully, intertwined."

Leslie Bianco | *Author and Founder*
In the Company of Prayer | companyofprayer.com

"Brian Sooy is a thoughtful, creative and seasoned follower of Christ. In **EntreWorship** we discover his passion—the fascinating crossroads where entrepreneurship and worship intersect.

John D. Beckett | *Chairman, The Beckett Companies*
Author: *Loving Monday* and *Mastering Monday*

"In an era in which we often worship entrepreneurs, Brian brings believers back to the right perspective on entrepreneurship. We create, because we are children of the Creator. *EntreWorship* hits the core of the things that many of struggle with in our ventures: isolation, feelings of inadequacy, impatience, busyness and more."

Todd Greer, PhD | *Vice President For Academic Affairs*
University of Mobile